Guess What!

Workbook 1

with Online Resources

American English

Susan Rivers

Series Editor: Lesley Koustaff

CAMBRIDGE
UNIVERSITY PRESS

CAMBRIDGE
UNIVERSITY PRESS & ASSESSMENT

Shaftesbury Road, Cambridge CB2 8EA, United Kingdom

One Liberty Plaza, 20th Floor, New York, NY 10006, USA

477 Williamstown Road, Port Melbourne, VIC 3207, Australia

314–321, 3rd Floor, Plot 3, Splendor Forum, Jasola District Centre, New Delhi – 110025, India

103 Penang Road, #05–06/07, Visioncrest Commercial, Singapore 238467

Cambridge University Press & Assessment is a department of the University of Cambridge.

We share the University's mission to contribute to society through the pursuit of education, learning and research at the highest international levels of excellence.

www.cambridge.org
Information on this title: www.cambridge.org/9781107556577

© Cambridge University Press & Assessment 2016

First published 2016

40 39 38 37 36 35 34 33 32 31

Printed in Poland by Opolgraf

A catalogue record for this publication is available from the British Library

ISBN   978-1-107-55657-7   Workbook with Online Resources Level 1
ISBN   978-1-107-55652-2   Student's Book Level 1
ISBN   978-1-107-55661-4   Teacher's Book with DVD Level 1
ISBN   978-1-107-55666-9   Class Audio CDs Level 1
ISBN   978-1-107-55669-0   Flashcards Level 1
ISBN   978-1-107-55671-3   Presentation Plus DVD-ROM Level 1
ISBN   978-1-107-55672-0   Teacher's Resource and Tests CD-ROM Levels 1–2

Additional resources for this publication at www.cambridge.org/guesswhatamericanenglish

Contents

Hello!

1 **Look and match.**

1

a

b

2

3

c

d

4

2 **Ask and answer with a friend.**

1 Hello, I'm Mandy. What's your name?

2 Hello, I'm Jack.

3 This is Penny.

4 Hello, Penny.

Listen and stick.

Listen and number.

1

5 Think **What's next? Draw a line.**

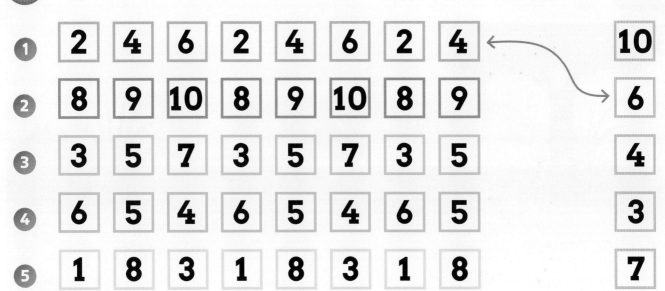

1 2 4 6 2 4 6 2 4 ← **10**

2 8 9 10 8 9 10 8 9 → **6**

3 3 5 7 3 5 7 3 5 **4**

4 6 5 4 6 5 4 6 5 **3**

5 1 8 3 1 8 3 1 8 **7**

6 CD1 11 **Listen and write the numbers in the pictures.**

1

2

3

4

7 **Listen and color.**

1

2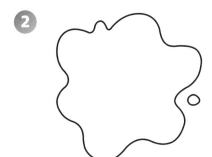

3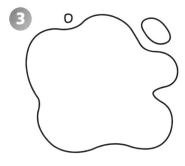

4

5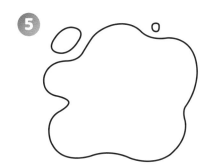

6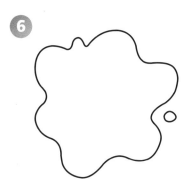

8  **Look. Then draw and say.**

1

2

How old are you?

What's your favorite color?

I'm …

My favorite color's …

My picture dictionary Go to page 84: Check the words you know and trace.

Grammar **7**

9 CD1 16 **Listen and check ✓.**

1

2

3

4

10 **What's missing? Look and draw. Then stick.**

a

b

c

I'm curious.

11 **Trace the letters.**

A pink and
purple panda.

12 CD1 19 **Listen and circle the *p* words.**

1

2

3

4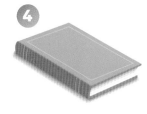

What **color** is it?

1 CD1 21 **Listen and color.**

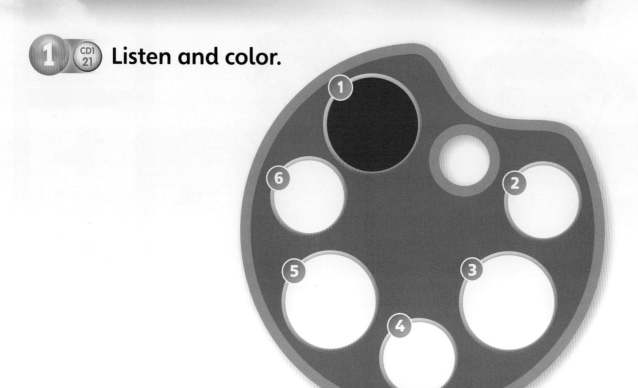

2 **Look and color.**

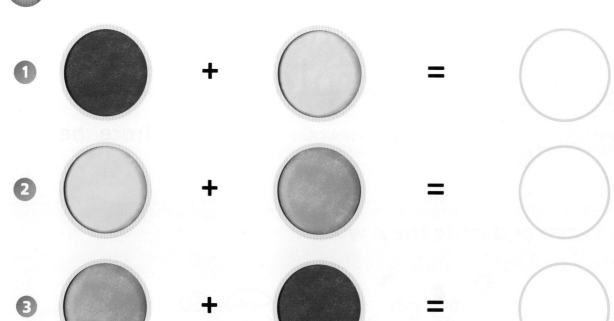

Evaluation

1 Follow the lines. Then trace and say.

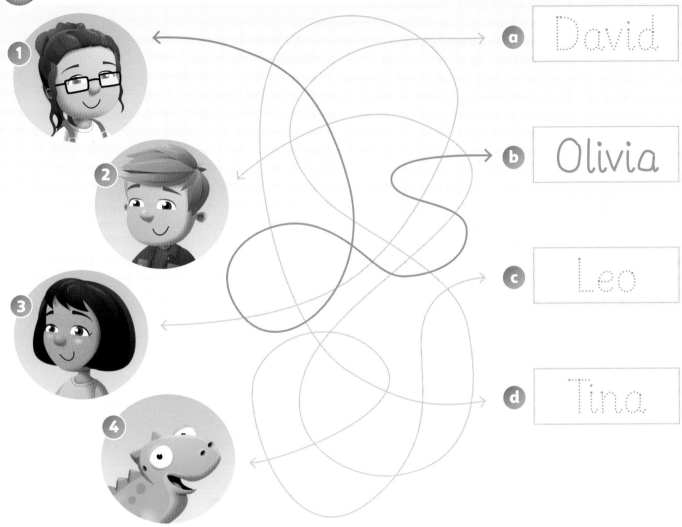

a David

b Olivia

c Leo

d Tina

2 What's your favorite part? Use your stickers.

story   song   video

3 Puzzle Trace the color.

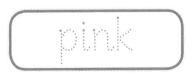

pink

Then go to page 93 and color the Hello! unit pieces.

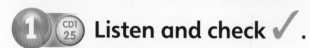

1 School

1 (CD1 25) **Listen and check ✓.**

1	2	3	4
a ✓	**a** ☐	**a** ☐	**a** ☐
b ☐	**b** abcde ☐	**b** ☐	**b** ☐

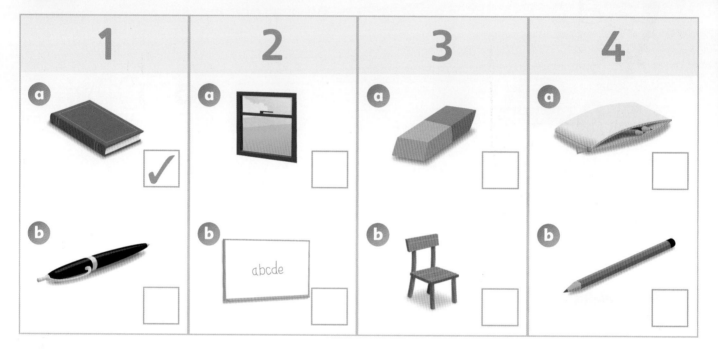

2 **Look and match.**

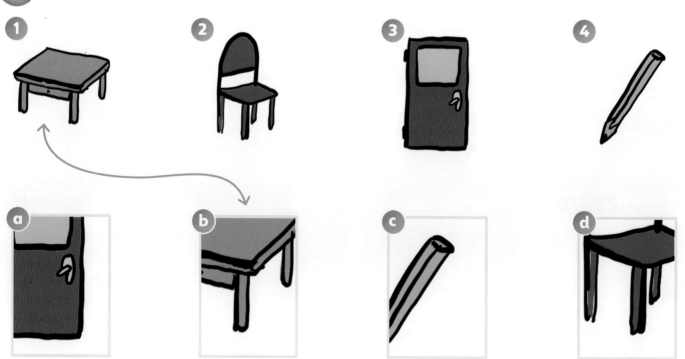

3 (CD1 27) 🏷 **Listen and stick.**

1

2

3

4

5

4 (Think) **What's next? Draw a line.**

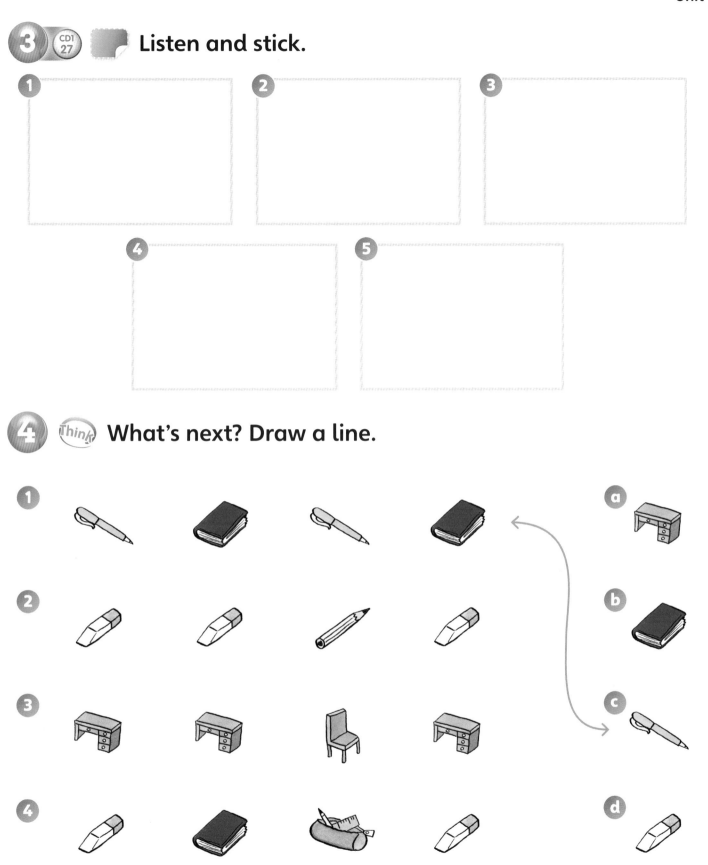

My picture dictionary → Go to page 85: Check the words you know and trace.

Vocabulary **13**

5 Look and count. Write the number.

2

6 (About Me) Ask and answer about your classroom.

How many erasers can you see?   Three.

7 CD1 32 **Listen and check ✓ or put an ✗.**

1

✗

2

3

4

8 Think **Circle the different one.**

1
 a
 b
c
d

2
 a
 b
c
d

What's missing? Look and draw. Then stick.

I'm friendly.

11 **Trace the letters.**

A bear with
a blue book.

12 Listen and circle the *b* words.

1

2

3

4

What material is it?

1 Look and match.

2 (CD1 39) Listen and check ✓.

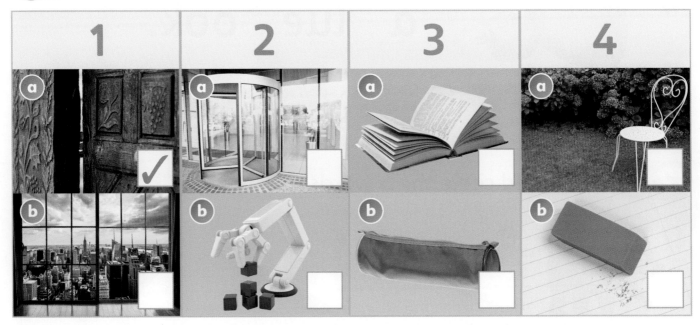

Evaluation

1 **Look and trace. Then say.**

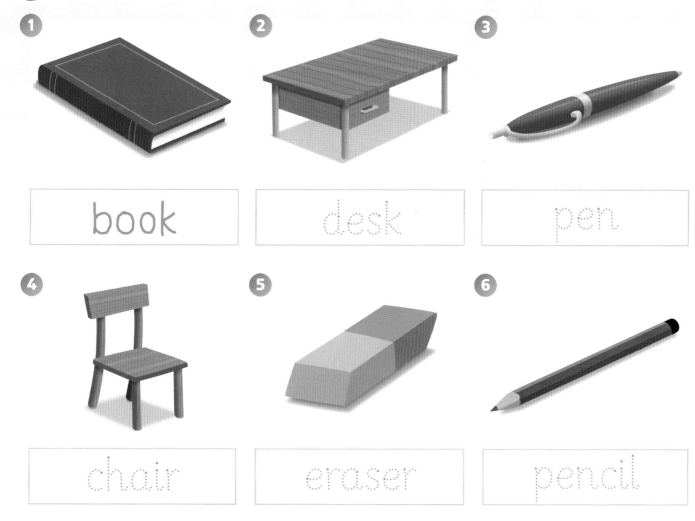

1 book

2 desk

3 pen

4 chair

5 eraser

6 pencil

2 **What's your favorite part? Use your stickers.**

story   song   video

3 Puzzle **Trace the color.**

red

Then go to page 93 and color the Unit 1 pieces.

Toys

1 CD1 43 Listen and check ✓.

1	2	3	4
a [✓]	**a** [ ]	**a** [ ]	**a** [ ]
b [ ]	**b** [ ]	**b** [ ]	**b** [ ]

2 Look, match, and say.

1 kite.

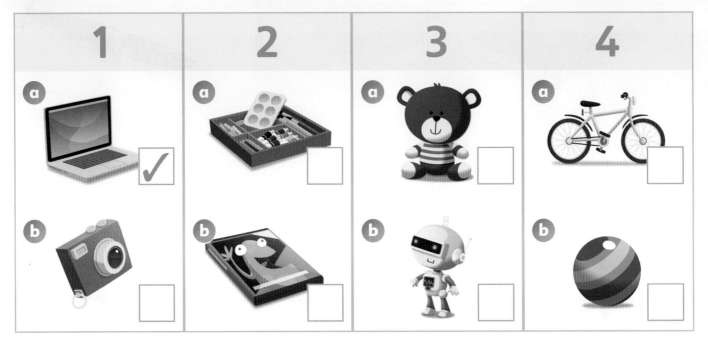

3 CD1 45 Listen and stick.

1

2

3

4

5

4 Think Look and circle the toys.

My picture dictionary → Go to page 86: Check the words you know and trace.

5 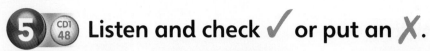 **Listen and check ✓ or put an ✗.**

1 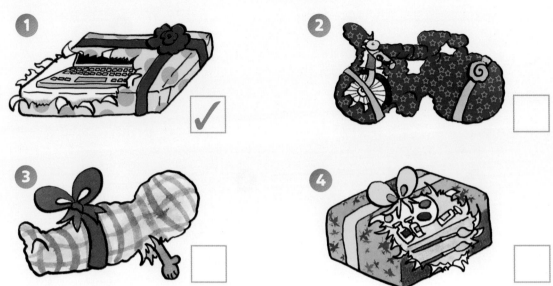 ✓

2 ☐

3 ☐

4 ☐

6 (About Me) **Draw your favorite toy and say.**

What's this?

It's a ...

7 **Listen and number the pictures.**

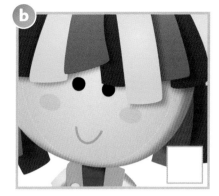

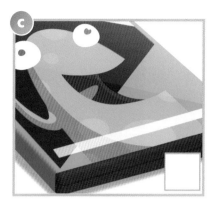

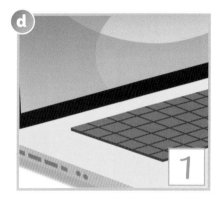

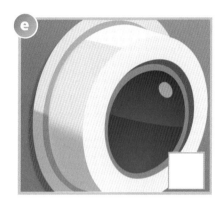

8 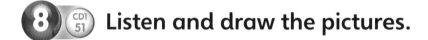 **Listen and draw the pictures.**

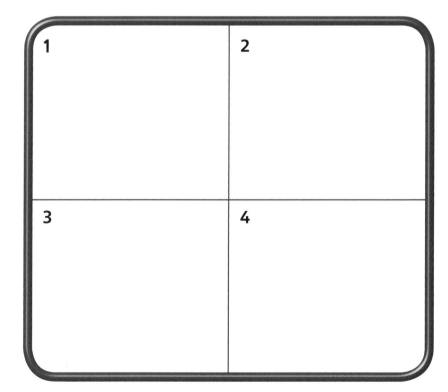

1

a ✓

b

2

a

b

3

a

b

4

a

b

10 **What's missing? Look and draw. Then stick.**

I'm polite. ☺

11 **Trace the letters.**

A turtle with two teddy bears.

12 CD1 56 **Listen and circle the *t* words.**

Is it electric?

1 (CD1 58) **Listen and check ✓ (electric) or put an ✗ (not electric).**

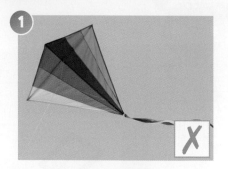

✗

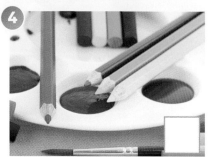

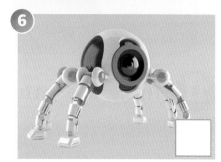

2 **Look at Activity 1 and draw.**

Electric

Not electric

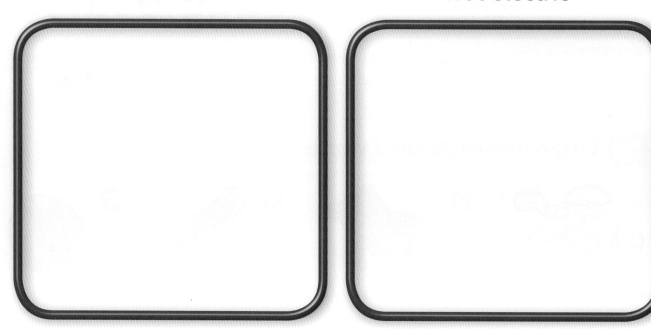

Evaluation

1 Look and trace. Then say.

1

kite

2
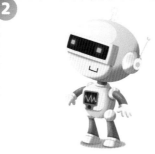

robot

3

ball

4

bike

5

doll

6

camera

2  What's your favorite part? Use your stickers.

story   song   video

3 **Puzzle** Trace the color.

green

Then go to page 93 and color the Unit 2 pieces.

Review Units 1 and 2

1 Look and say. Find and circle.

2 CD1 60 **Listen and number the pictures.**

a

b

c

d

1

e

f

7

3 Family

1 Trace the words and match.

1 mom

2 dad

3 sister

4 brother

5 grandma

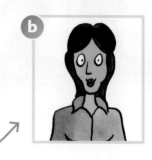

2 Look and write the number.

1 cousin   2 uncle   3 grandpa   4 aunt

3 CD2 07 **Listen and stick.**

1	2	3	4	5

4 Think **Read, look, and check ✓.**

1 dad

☐ ☐ ✓

2 aunt

☐ ☐ ☐

3 grandma

☐ ☐ ☐

4 brother

☐ ☐ ☐

 My picture dictionary → **Go to page 87: Check the words you know and trace.**

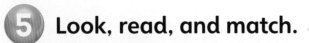

5 Look, read, and match.

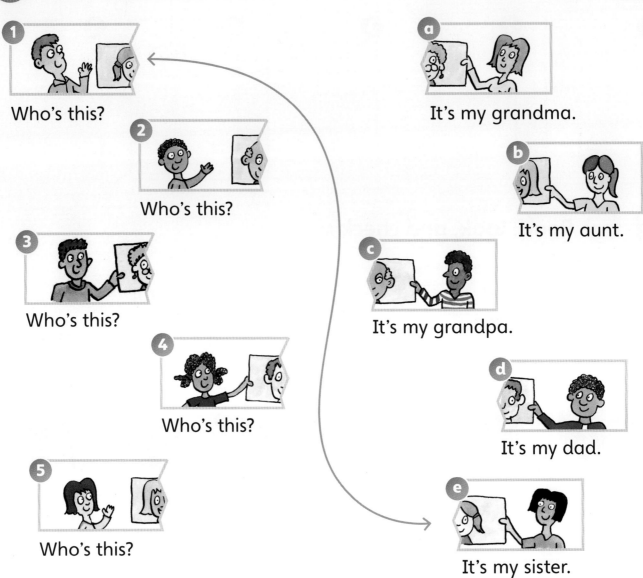

1 Who's this?

2 Who's this?

3 Who's this?

4 Who's this?

5 Who's this?

a It's my grandma.

b It's my aunt.

c It's my grandpa.

d It's my dad.

e It's my sister.

6 (About Me) Draw a member of your family. Then ask and answer with a friend.

Who's this?

It's my ... .

7 CD2 12 **Listen, read, and check ✓.**

1

my brother ☐

my cousin ✓

2

my mom ☐

my aunt ☐

3

my mom ☐

my grandma ☐

4

my sister ☐

my cousin ☐

5

my cousin ☐

my aunt ☐

6

my dad ☐

my uncle ☐

8 **Look, read, and circle the correct word.**

1 Who's **this** / (**that**)?
It's my uncle.

2 Who's **this** / **that**?
It's my cousin.

3 Who's **this** / **that**?
It's my grandpa.

4 Who's **this** / **that**?
It's my sister.

9  Listen, look, and match.

1

2

3

4

5

6

a

b

c

d

e

f

What's missing? Look and draw. Then stick.

I love my family.

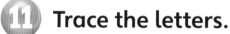 **Trace the letters.**

A dolphin in a red desk.

 **Listen and circle the *d* words.**

  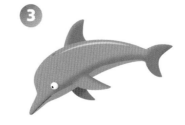 

What continent is it?

1 **Listen and write the number.**

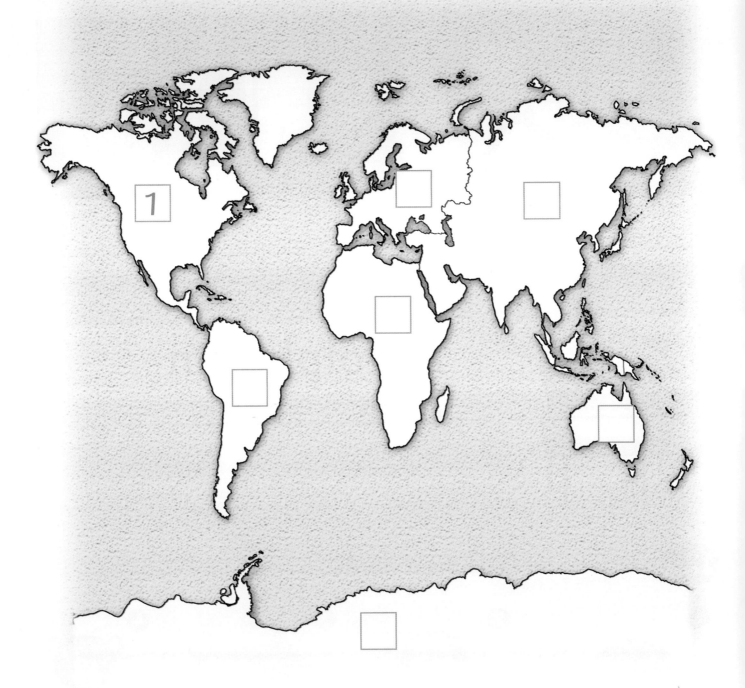

2 **Look at the map again. Listen and color.**

Evaluation

1 **Read and trace. Then circle and say.**

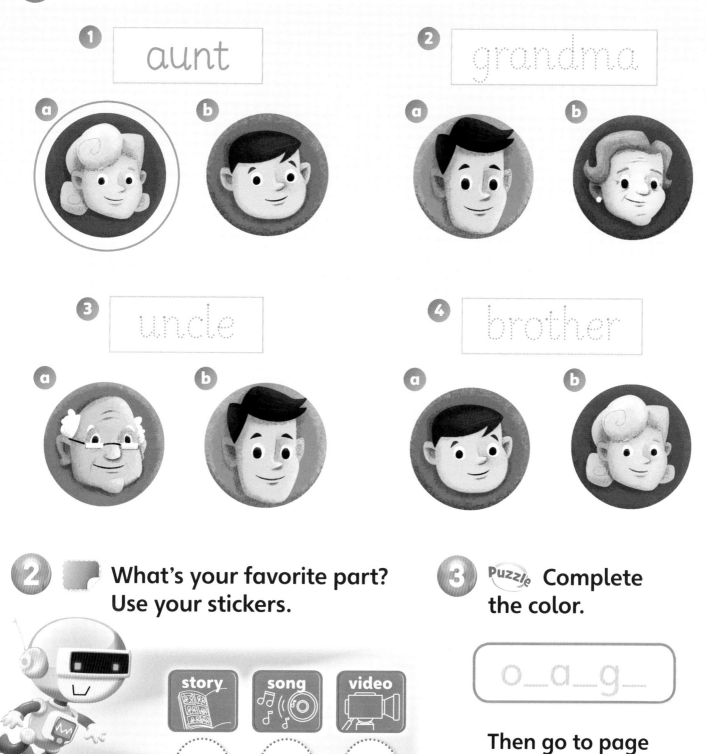

1 aunt

2 grandma

3 uncle

4 brother

2 What's your favorite part? Use your stickers.

story   song   video

3 Puzzle Complete the color.

o_a_g_

Then go to page 93 and color the Unit 3 pieces.

1 Look at the picture and write the letter.

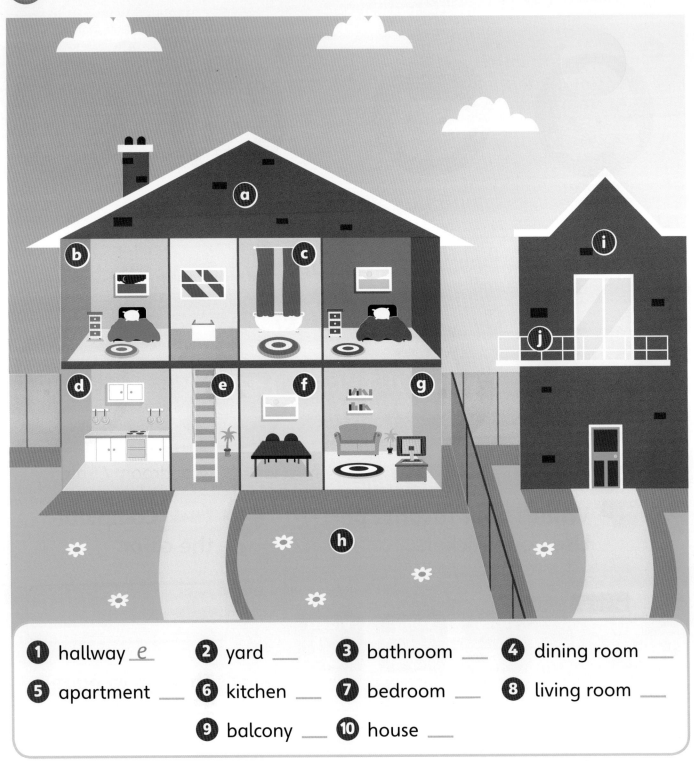

1 hallway _e_   **2** yard ___   **3** bathroom ___   **4** dining room ___

5 apartment ___   **6** kitchen ___   **7** bedroom ___   **8** living room ___

9 balcony ___   **10** house ___

2 Listen and stick.

1 | 2 | 3

4 | 5 | 6

3 Look, read, and circle the correct word.

1

(kitchen) / dining room

2

hallway / living room

3

bedroom / balcony

4

kitchen / bathroom

5

hallway / yard

6

balcony / dining room

My picture dictionary Go to page 88: Check the words you know and trace.

Look, read, and match.

1

Where's your aunt?

a

I'm in the yard.

2

Where's your cousin?

b

She's in the hallway.

3

Where's your mom?

c

She's in the bathroom.

4

Where are you?

d

He's in the bedroom.

  Draw yourself. Ask and answer with a friend.

Where are you?

I'm in …

6 **Listen and write the number.**

1   **2**  **3**  **4**  **5**

7 **Draw the objects in the picture. Ask and answer.**

Where's the … ?   It's … .

8 🎵 CD2 32 Listen and number.

9 **What's missing? Look and draw. Then stick.**

I take care of things.

10 **Trace the letters.**

An ant with an apple.

11 CD2 35 **Listen and circle the *a* words.**

1 2 3 4

What shape is it?

1 Look and color the shapes.

2 What's next? Match, then draw and color the shapes.

square

triangle

circle

Evaluation

1 Read and trace. Then circle and say.

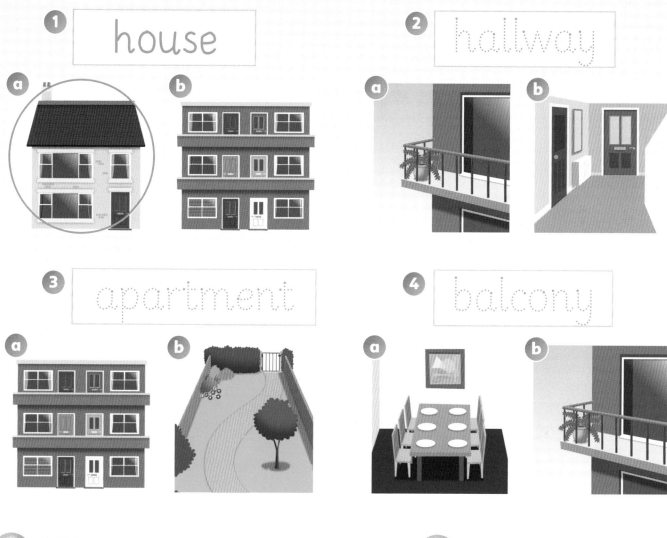

1. house
2. hallway
3. apartment
4. balcony

2 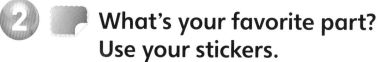 What's your favorite part? Use your stickers.

3 Puzzle Complete the color.

y_l_o_

Then go to page 93 and color the Unit 4 pieces.

Review Units 3 and 4

1 Write the words and match.

1	2	3	4	5	6	7	8	9	10	11	12	13	14	15	16	17
u	a	t	b	s	c	r	d	o	e	n	g	m	h	k	i	y

1 b r o t h e r

4 7 9 3 14 10 7

2 _____ _____ _____ _____ _____ _____ _____

15 16 3 6 14 10 11

3 _____ _____ _____ _____ _____ _____ _____

12 7 2 11 8 13 2

4 _____ _____ _____ _____

17 2 7 8

5 _____ _____ _____

8 2 8

6 _____ _____ _____ _____ _____

14 9 1 5 10

a

b

c

d

e

f

2 **Read and match the questions with the answers.**

1 Where's the computer? _c_   a She's in the living room.
2 Is that your cousin? _____   b No, it isn't. It's my sister.
3 Who's that? _____   c It's on the desk.
4 Where's your mom? _____   d It's my sister.

3 **Circle the correct words and write.**

mom   bedroom   grandma   ~~under~~

1

What's / (Where's) the doll?
It's _under_ the bed.

2

Who's / Where's this?
It's my _____ .

3

Who / Where are you?
I'm in my _____ .

4

Is that / Who's your aunt?
No, it isn't.
It's my _____ .

47

1 Read and circle the correct word.

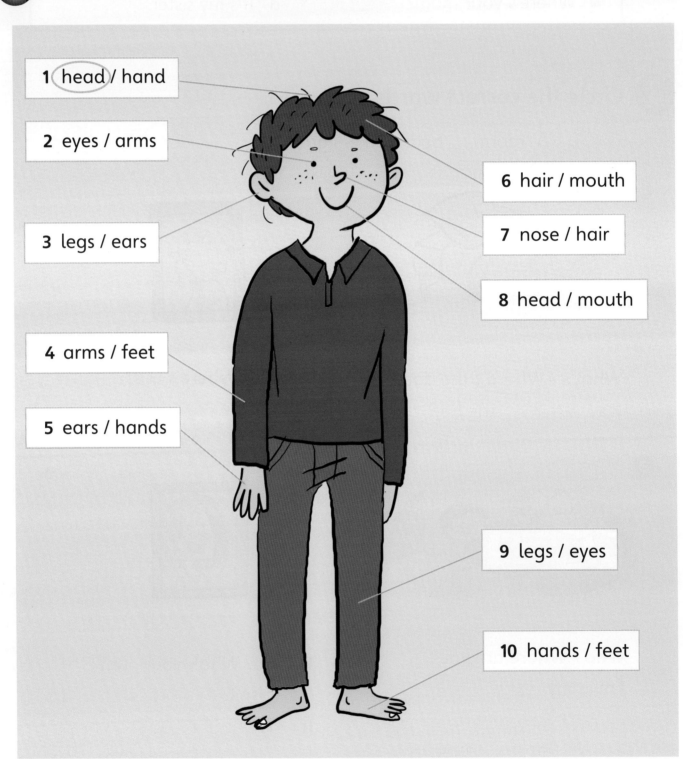

1 (head) / hand

2 eyes / arms

3 legs / ears

4 arms / feet

5 ears / hands

6 hair / mouth

7 nose / hair

8 head / mouth

9 legs / eyes

10 hands / feet

2   **Listen and stick.**

1

2

3

4

5

6

3 **Look at the picture. Find and circle the words.**

h	e	a	d	e	p	n
l	e	g	l	a	l	o
h	h	k	o	r	j	s
a	a	e	r	t	y	e
i	r	w	h	a	n	d
r	m	o	u	t	h	n
q	n	v	f	e	e	t

My picture dictionary → Go to page 89: Check the words you know and trace.

4 **Listen and check ✓.**

5 **Think** **What's different? Circle the word.**

(eyes) / ears

feet / hands

legs / arms

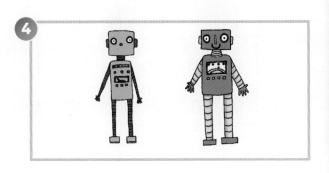

mouth / nose

6 Look, read, and check ✓ .

1

Do you have hair?

☐ Yes, I do. ✓ No, I don't.

2

Do you have two arms?

☐ Yes, I do. ☐ No, I don't.

3

Do you have four legs?

☐ Yes, I do. ☐ No, I don't.

4

Do you have one nose?

☐ Yes, I do. ☐ No, I don't.

7 (About Me) **Draw a robot. Then complete the sentences.**

I have _____

_____ .

I don't have _____

_____ .

8 CD2 48 Listen and check ✓.

1

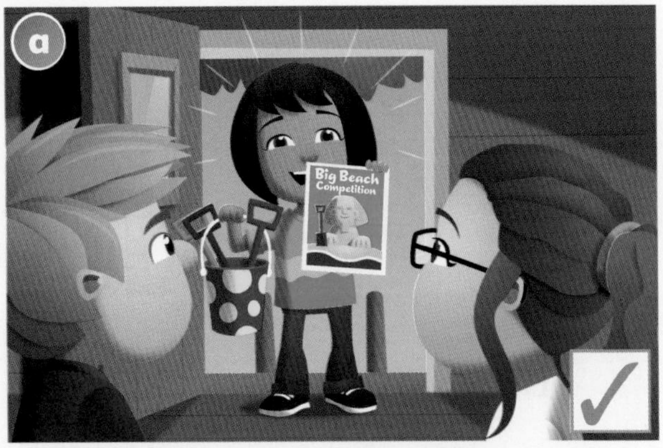

a
Big Beach Competition
✓

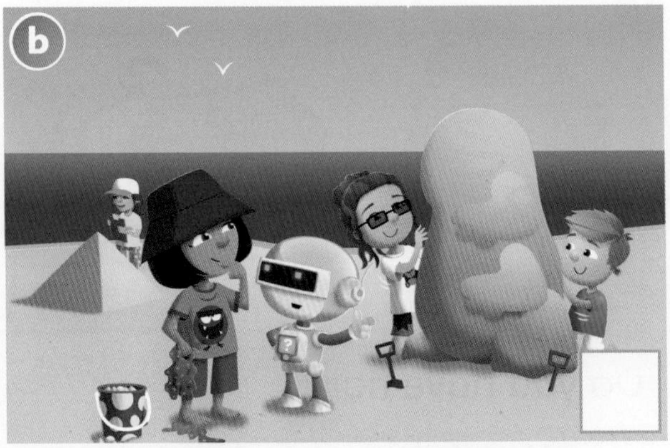

b

2

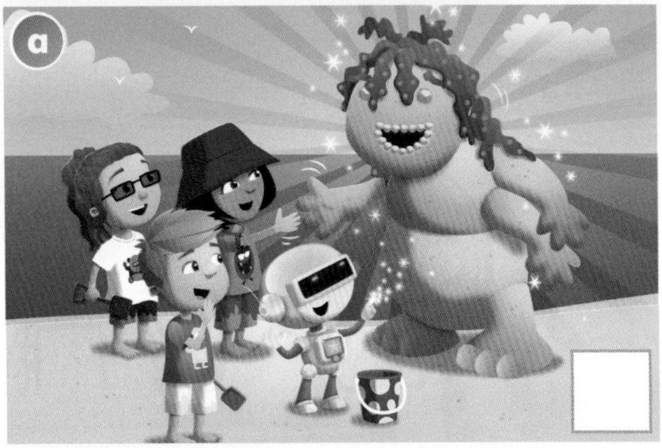

a

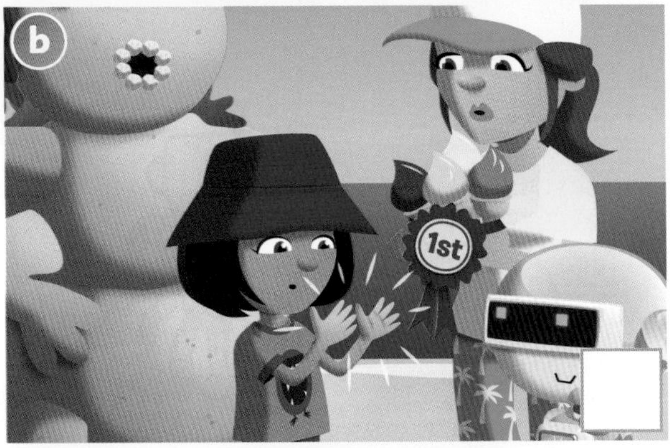

b
1st

3

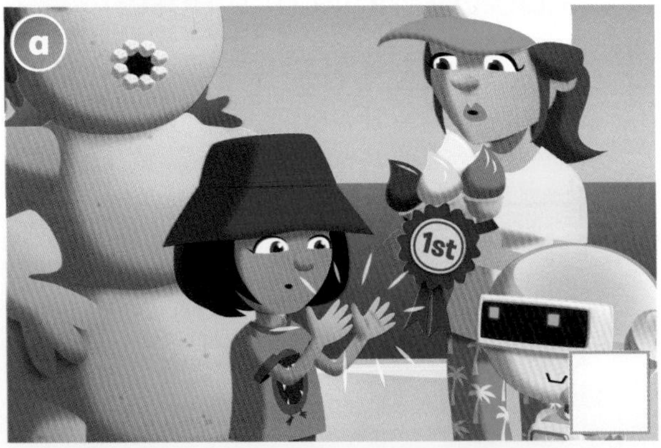

a
1st

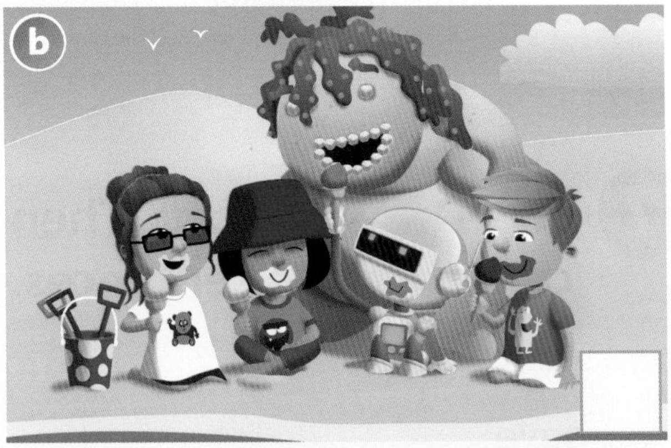

b

4

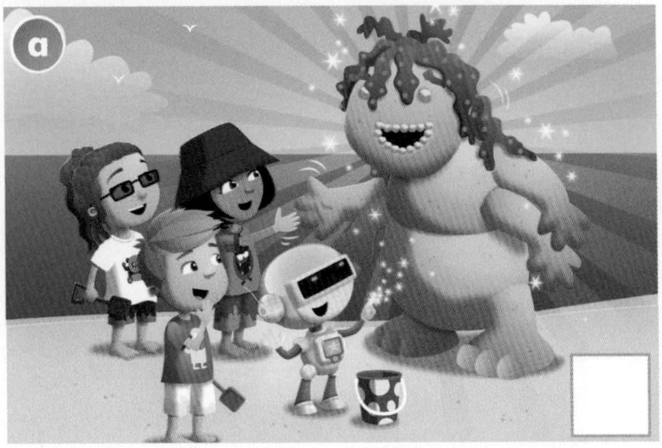

a

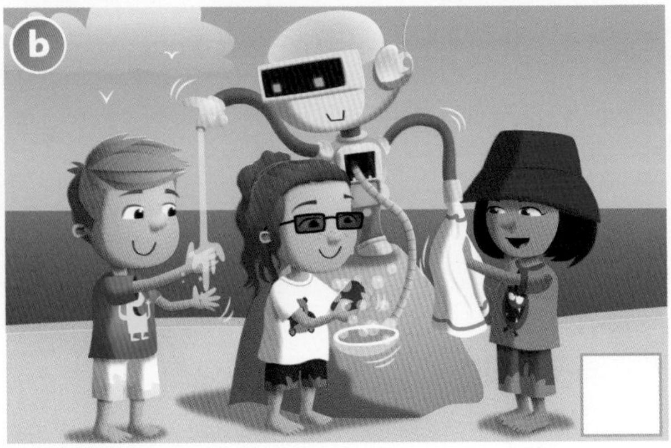

b

9 **What's missing? Look and draw. Then stick.**

I'm clean.

a

b

c

10 **Trace the letters.**

An iguana
with pink ink.

11 CD2 51 **Listen and circle the *i* words.**

1

2

3

4

What sense is it?

1 Look, read, and match.

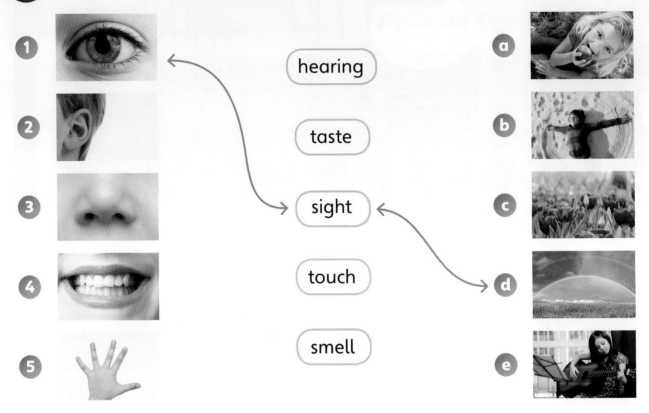

1 — sight

hearing

taste

sight

touch

smell

a
b
c
d
e

2 Look and check ✓.

	👁	👂	👃	😬	✋
	✓				

Evaluation

1 Look, match, and trace. Then read and say.

head

feet

ears

nose

2 What's your favorite part? Use your stickers.

story   song   video

3 Puzzle Complete the color.

b_u_

Then go to page 93 and color the Unit 5 pieces.

6 Food

1 Look and write the word.

1  k m l i

milk

2  p e a l p

_____

3  g e g

_____

4  c e h s e e

_____

5  a e w r t

_____

6  a a a n n b

_____

2 Complete the words and match.

1 jui_c_e   2 o__ange   3 b__ead   4 c__ick__n

a    **b**    **c**    **d**

3 **Listen and stick.**

1	2

3	4

4 **Look and write the words.**

cheese   an apple   juice   bread   water
a banana   an egg   an orange   chicken   milk

We eat ...
1 cheese
2
3
4
5
6
7

We drink ...
1
2
3

My picture dictionary → Go to page 90: Check the words you know and trace.

5 **CD3 09** **Listen and check ✓ or put an ✗.**

1				✓	✗
2					
3					
4					

6 **Look, read, and circle.**

1  I **like** / **don't like** juice.

2 I **like** / **don't like** oranges.

3  I **like** / **don't like** bread.

4  I **like** / **don't like** water.

5  I **like** / **don't like** apples.

6  I **like** / **don't like** eggs.

7 **Look, read, and check ✓.**

1

Do you like bread?

✓ Yes, I do. ☐ No, I don't.

2

Do you like eggs?

☐ Yes, I do. ☐ No, I don't.

3

Do you like bananas?

☐ Yes, I do. ☐ No, I don't.

4

Do you like juice?

☐ Yes, I do. ☐ No, I don't.

8 **(About Me)** **Look and answer the questions with *Yes, I do* or *No, I don't*.**

1  Do you like chicken?

_____ .

2 Do you like milk?

_____ .

3 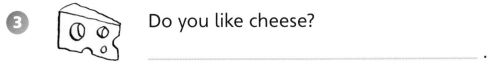 Do you like cheese?

_____ .

4  Do you like bananas?

_____ .

10 **What's missing? Look and draw. Then stick.**

I'm patient.

11 **Trace the letters.**

An elephant with ten eggs.

12 **Listen and circle the e words.**

1

2

3

4

Where is **food** from?

1 Look and check ✓ or put an ✗.

Plants

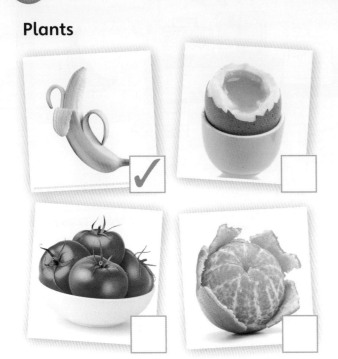

Animals

2 Look, read, and circle.

1

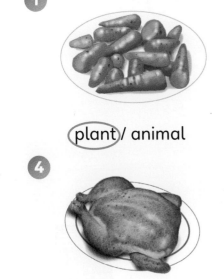

(plant) / animal

2

plant / animal

3

plant / animal

4

plant / animal

5

plant / animal

6

plant / animal

Evaluation

1 **Look, match, and write. Then read and say.**

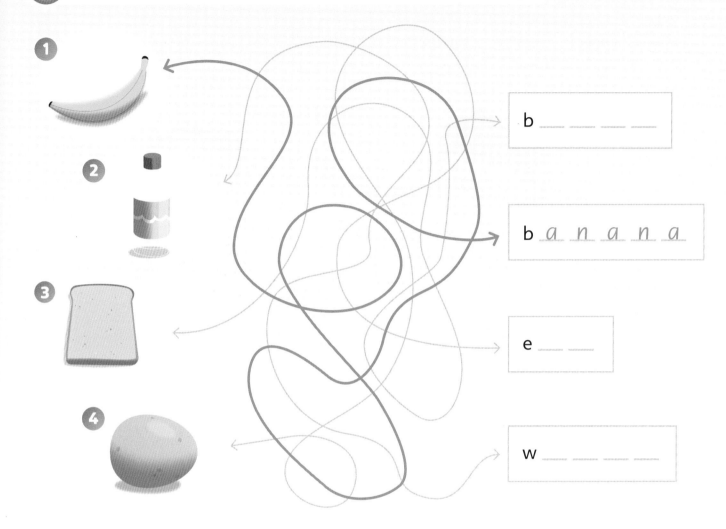

b _ _ _ _ _

b a n a n a

e _ _ _

w _ _ _ _ _

2 **What's your favorite part? Use your stickers.**

story   song   video

3 **Puzzle Write the color.**

p e u l r p _ _ _ _ _

Then go to page 93 and color the Unit 6 pieces.

Review Units 5 and 6

1 Look and write.

cheese	~~arms~~	water	mouth
bread	legs	orange	nose

1 _arms_		**2**	
3		**4**	
5		**6**	
7		**8**	

2 Read and match.

1	I like		**a**	like juice.
2	I have		**b**	two ears.
3	I don't		**c**	chicken.
4	I don't have		**d**	two heads.

3 Write the question. Then check ✓.

1

you / three / Do / have / hands / ?

Do you have three hands?

☐ Yes, I do. ✓ No, I don't.

2

like / eggs / you / Do / ?

_____

☐ Yes, I do. ☐ No, I don't.

3

have / two / you / Do / ears / ?

_____

☐ Yes, I do. ☐ No, I don't.

4

you / Do / milk / like / ?

_____

☐ Yes, I do. ☐ No, I don't.

7 Actions

1 **Look, read, and circle the word.**

1

swim / (sing)

2

climb / paint

3

dance / draw

4

ride a bike / play soccer

2 **Look at the pictures. Find and circle the words.**

1

2

3

4

5

6

runswimjumppaintclimb(dance)

3 CD3 22  **Listen and stick.**

1

2

3

4

5

6

4 Think **Read and circle the object.**

1 dance

2 draw

3 sing

4 swim

My picture dictionary ➜ Go to page 91: Check the words you know and trace.

5 CD3 25 **Listen and circle the picture.**

1

2

3

4

6 **Look and write *can* or *can't*.**

1 I _can_ run.

2 I _____ draw.

3 I _____ climb.

4 I _____ dance.

7 **Look, read, and check ✓.**

Can you swim?

☐ Yes, I can. ✓ No, I can't.

Can you jump?

☐ Yes, I can. ☐ No, I can't.

Can you ride a bike?

☐ Yes, I can. ☐ No, I can't.

Can you dance?

☐ Yes, I can. ☐ No, I can't.

8 **Complete the chart. Ask three friends and check ✓.**

Name			
1 _Me_			
2			
3			
4			

Can you sing? Yes, I can. / No, I can't.

Listen and number.

1

10 **What's missing? Look and draw. Then stick.**

I help my friends.

11 **Trace the letters.**

An umbrella bird can jump.

12 CD3 31 **Listen and circle the *u* words.**

 1

 2

 3

 4

What's the number?

1 **Think and write the answer. Then color.**

1. 1 + 1 = [2] red   2. 2 + 4 = [ ] blue

3. 3 + 6 = [ ] orange   4. 10 − 2 = [ ] purple

5. 5 − 2 = [ ] green   6. 8 − 4 = [ ] yellow

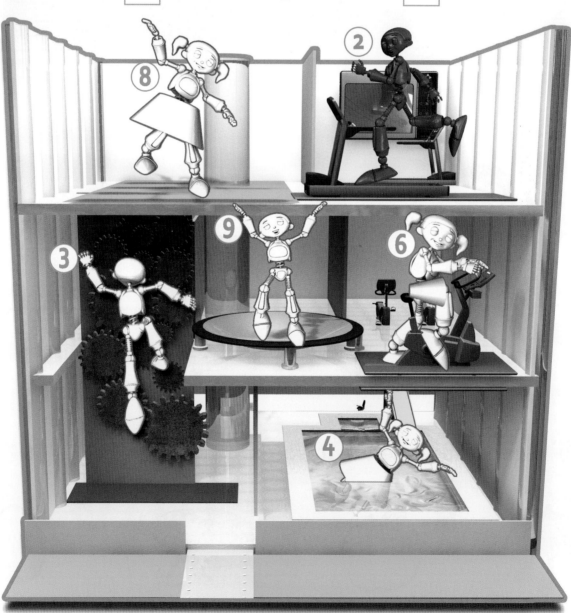

Evaluation

1 Look and write the words. Then read and say.

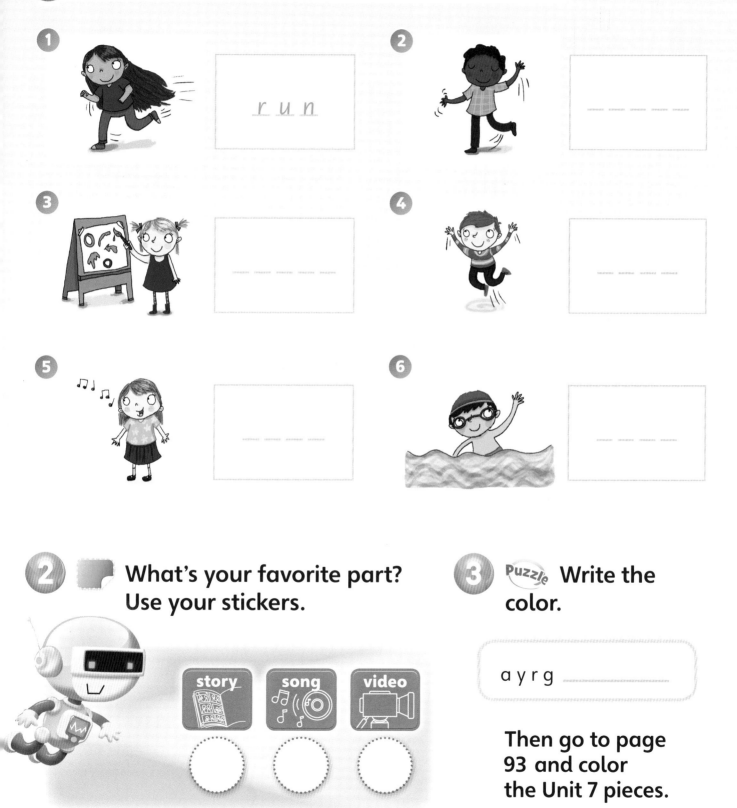

1 r u n

2

3

4

5

6

2 What's your favorite part? Use your stickers.

story   song   video

3 Puzzle Write the color.

a y r g

Then go to page 93 and color the Unit 7 pieces.

1 **Look and match.**

a crocodile   **b** giraffe   **c** spider   **d** elephant

2 **Look and write the word.**

1    n l o i
lion

2    b e r z a

3    i d b r

4    o i p h p

5    m y o e k n

6    e a k n s

3 CD3 37 **Listen and stick.**

1	2	3
4	5	6

4 Think **Write the words. Circle the animals with four legs.**

snake   spider   bird   ~~zebra~~   elephant   giraffe   hippo   lion

1 zebra

2

3

4

5

6

7

8

My picture dictionary → **Go to page 92: Check the words you know and trace.**

5 Look and match the opposites.

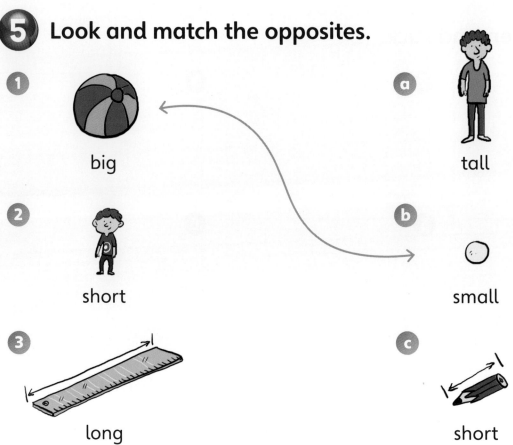

1. big
2. short
3. long

a. tall
b. small
c. short

6 Look, read, and complete the sentences.

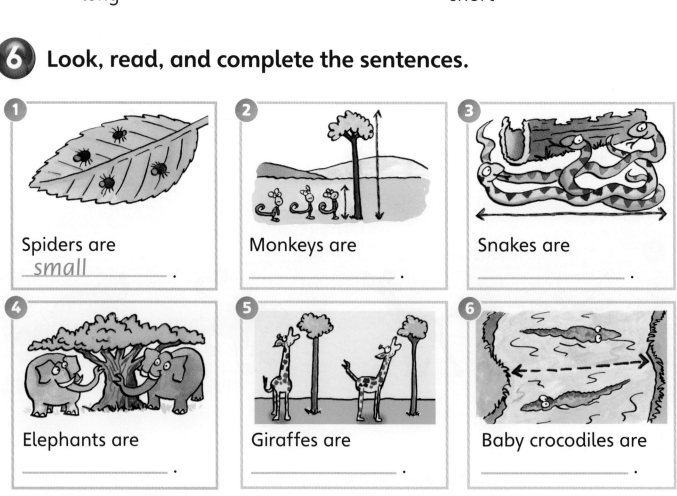

1. Spiders are _small_ .

2. Monkeys are _____ .

3. Snakes are _____ .

4. Elephants are _____ .

5. Giraffes are _____ .

6. Baby crocodiles are _____ .

7 **Look and read. Circle the correct sentences.**

| Spiders have wings. | Elephants have long trunks. |

| Hippos have long necks. | Monkeys have long tails. |

8 **Look and write.**

big teeth   long tails   ~~small wings~~   long necks   short legs

1 Birds have _small_ _wings_ .

2 Zebras have _____ .

3 Hippos have _____ .

4 Giraffes have _____ .

5 Birds have _____ .

9 **Ask and answer with a friend.**

What are your favorite animals?   Elephants.

10 CD3 43 Listen and check ✓.

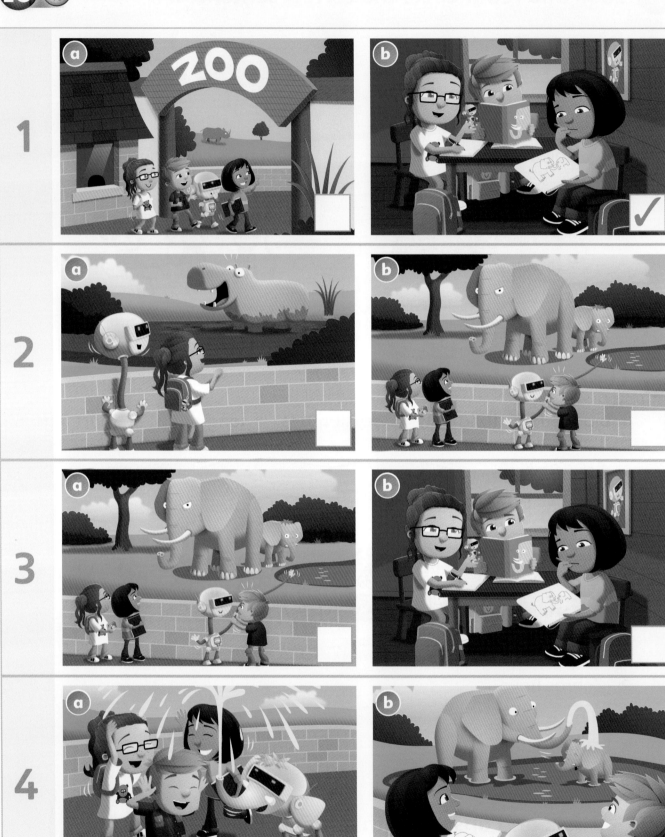

11 **What's missing? Look and draw. Then stick.**

I respect animals.

12 **Trace the letters.**

An octopus in an orange box.

13 CD3 46 **Listen and circle the o words.**

1

2

3

4

How do **animals** move?

1 **Read and complete. Then number the pictures.**

slither   ~~walk~~   fly   walk

1 An elephant can __*walk*__ .   **2** A snake can _____ .
3 A bird can _____ .   **4** A giraffe can _____ .

a

b

c

d

1

2 **Look at Activity 1 and circle the answers.**

1 Can a snake fly?   Yes, it can. / No, it can't.
2 Can an elephant walk?   Yes, it can. / No, it can't.
3 Can a bird fly?   Yes, it can. / No, it can't.
4 Can a giraffe slither?   Yes, it can. / No, it can't.

Evaluation

1 **Look and write the word. Then read and say.**

1

z e b r a

2

3

4

5

6

2 **What's your favorite part? Use your stickers.**

story

song

video

3 **Puzzle** **Write the color.**

l c k a b _____

Then go to page 93 and color the Unit 8 pieces.

Review Units 7 and 8

1 Look and write. Then draw number 9.

		9			
1	z	e	b	r	a
2		a		o	c	r
3 s		a			
4 j					
5		i		p	
6		n		e	
7	o		e		
8	a		n		

82

2 Look and write.

soccer	small	long necks	a bike	~~swim~~

1 Can you _swim_ ?

2 Birds are _____ .

3 I can play _____ .

4 Giraffes have _____ .

5 I can't ride _____ .

3 Look, read, and circle the words.

1

(**Snakes**) / **Spiders** are long.

2

I **can** / **can't** sing.

3

Hippos **have** / **don't have** short tails.

4

I can **draw** / **dance**.

Hello!

blue ☐

green ☐

orange ☐

pink ☐

purple ☐

red ☐

yellow ☐

1 School

board

book

chair

desk

door

pen

pencil

pencil case

eraser

window

② Toys

art set ball bike

camera computer computer doll
game

kite robot teddy
bear

aunt

brother

cousin

dad

grandma

grandpa

mom

sister

uncle

(4) At home

balcony

bathroom

bedroom

dining room

apartment

yard

hallway

house

kitchen

living room

5 My body

arms

ears

eyes

feet

head

hair

hands

legs

mouth

nose

(6) Food

apple   banana   bread

cheese   chicken   egg   juice

milk   orange   water

7 Actions

climb

dance

draw

jump

paint

play soccer

ride a bike

run

sing

swim

(8) Animals

bird

crocodile

elephant

giraffe

hippo

lion

monkey

snake

spider

zebra

My puzzle

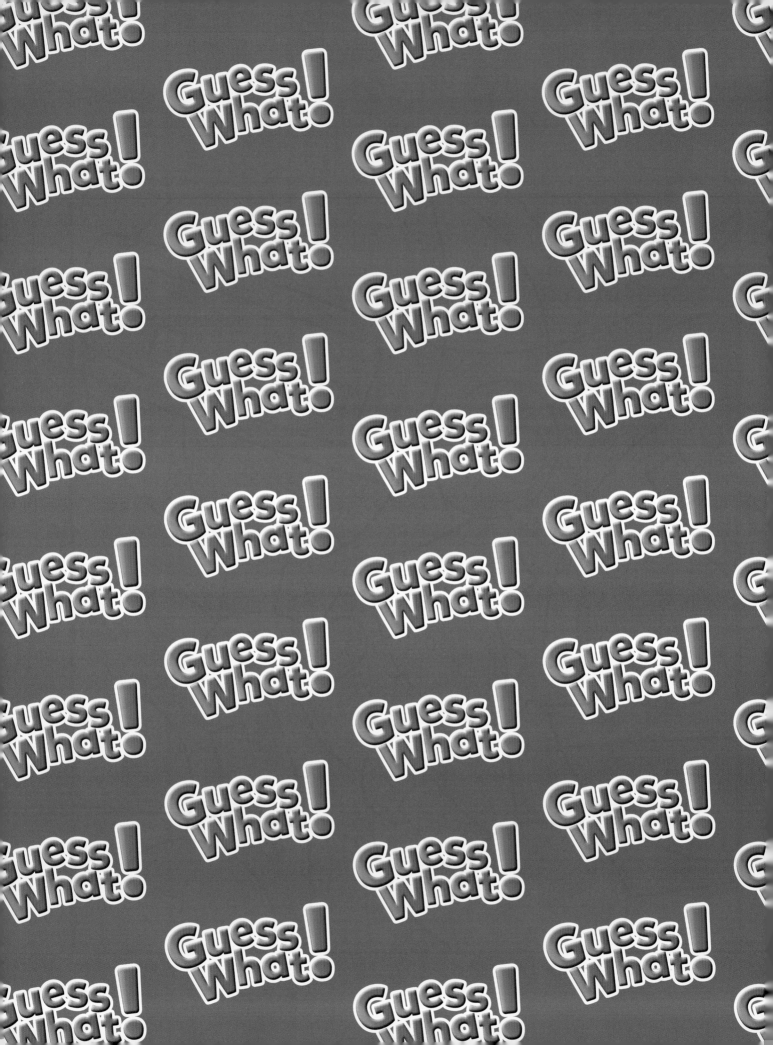